Me and My Piano
Duets book 1

Written, selected and edited by Fanny Waterman

Dear young pianist,

I hope you will enjoy playing these duets with a friend, your parent or teacher.

Here are a few tips to help you:

1 Don't always play the Primo part. In pieces where the Secondo part is marked Pupil/Teacher, you might like to swap around once you have learnt the Primo part.

2 Before you begin, count aloud a full bar's rest. Take it in turns to count in. If one of you goes wrong or gets lost, be prepared to start from any beat of any bar.

3 Watch your partner's hands and face every time you see this sign: ⌾⌾
It will help you to stay together at the beginnings and ends of pieces, at pauses, and at places where the music slows down or speeds up again.

4 Follow all the dynamics carefully. The Secondo part must never overpower the Primo.

Fanny Waterman.

FABER *ff* MUSIC

1 Do, do l'enfant do Secondo Pupil/teacher

Old French

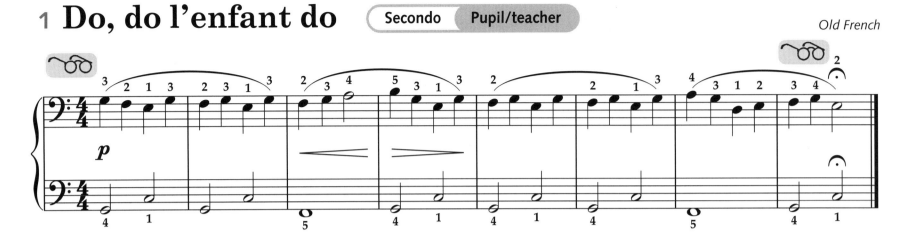

2 A, a, a, the summer's fled away Secondo Pupil/teacher

Traditional

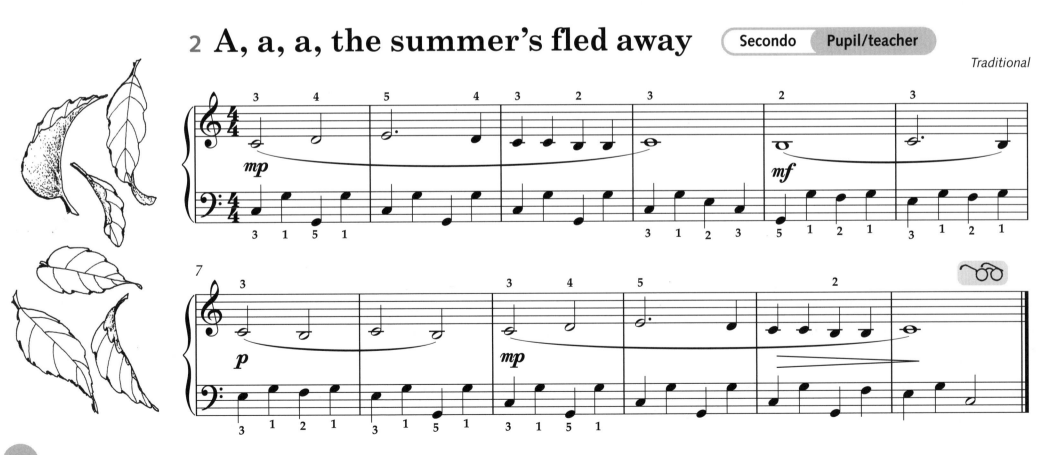

1 Do, do l'enfant do

Primo Pupil

Old French

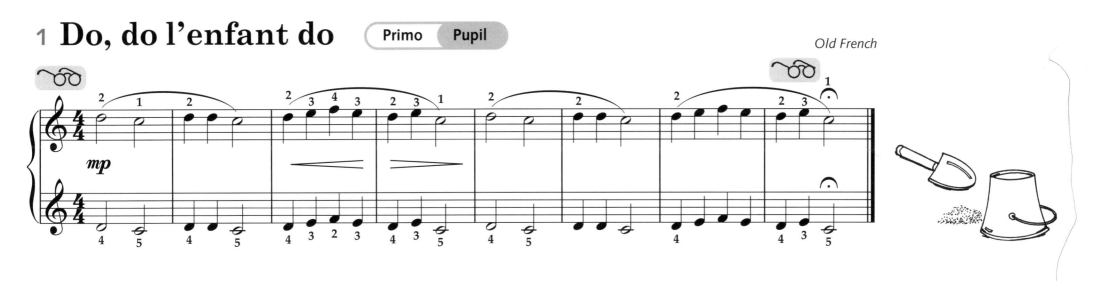

2 A, a, a, the summer's fled away

Primo Pupil

Traditional

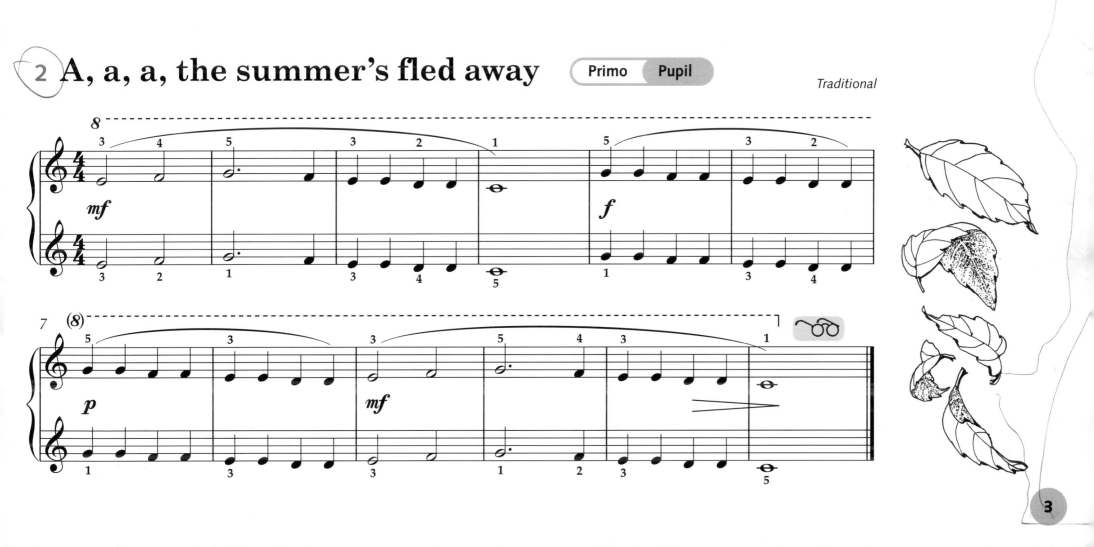

3

3 Twilight

Secondo | Teacher

Andante cantabile

Diabelli

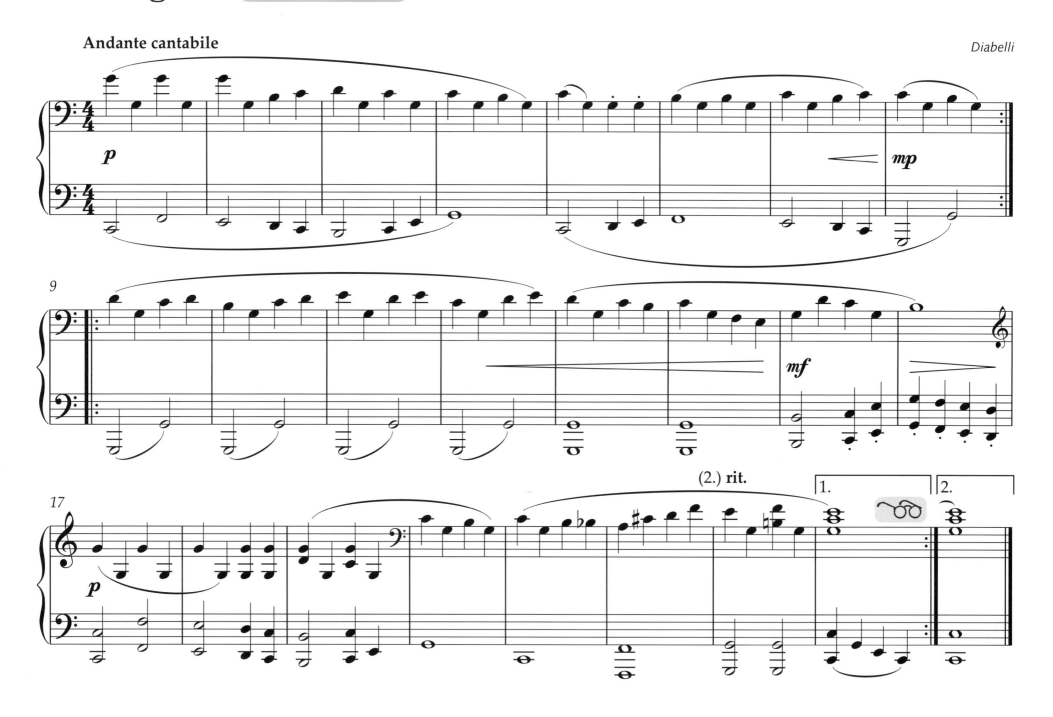

3 Twilight

Primo | Pupil

Diabelli

Andante cantabile

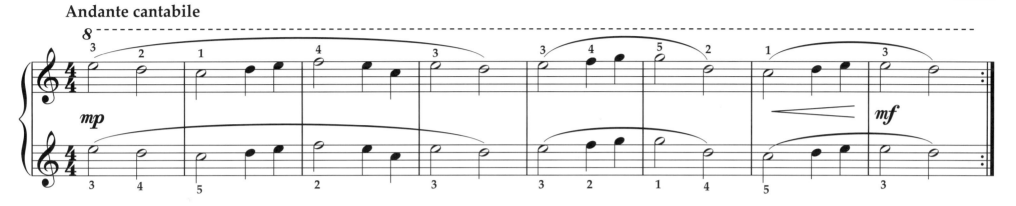

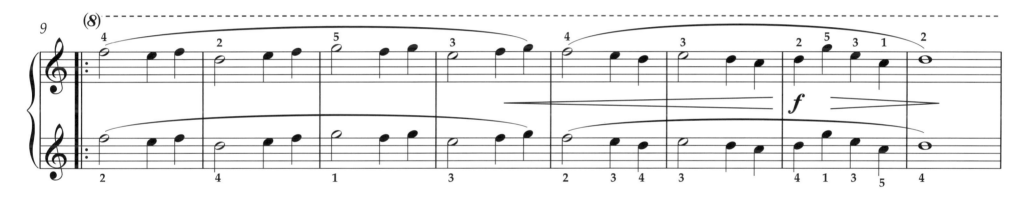

(2.) **rit.**

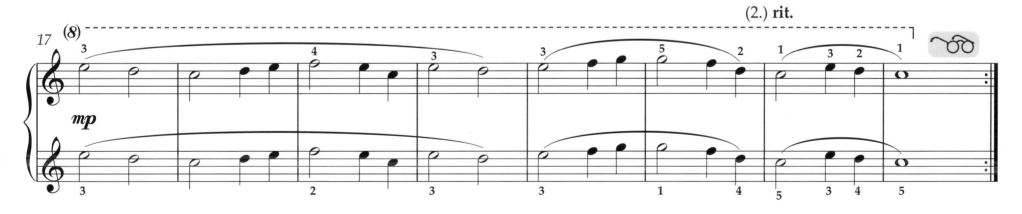

4 German song

Traditional

5 Ah! Vous dirai-je, maman

Mozart

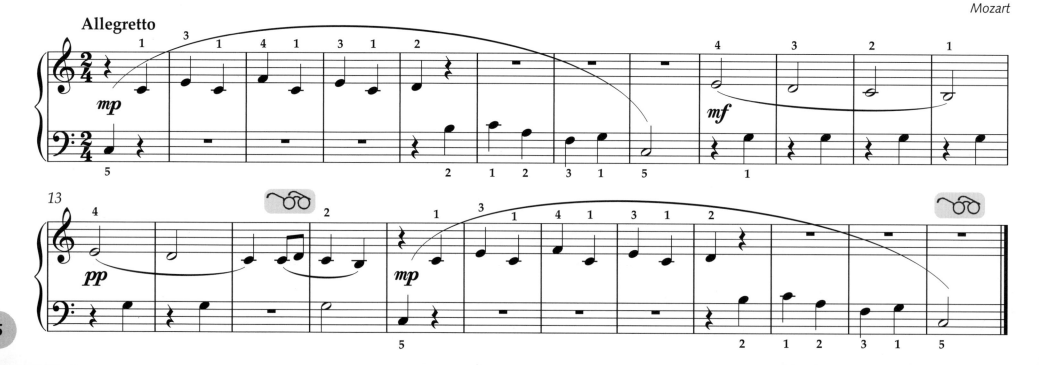

4 German song

Traditional

7.6.16

5 Ah! Vous dirai-je, maman

Primo Pupil

Mozart

6 Dreaming Secondo · Teacher

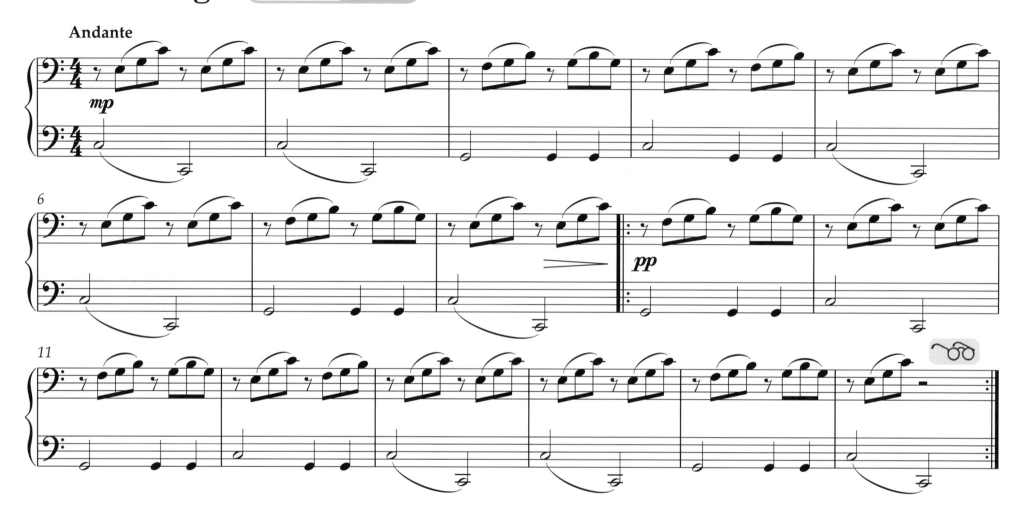

7 Little Cossack Secondo · Teacher

Traditional

6 Dreaming

Primo **Pupil**

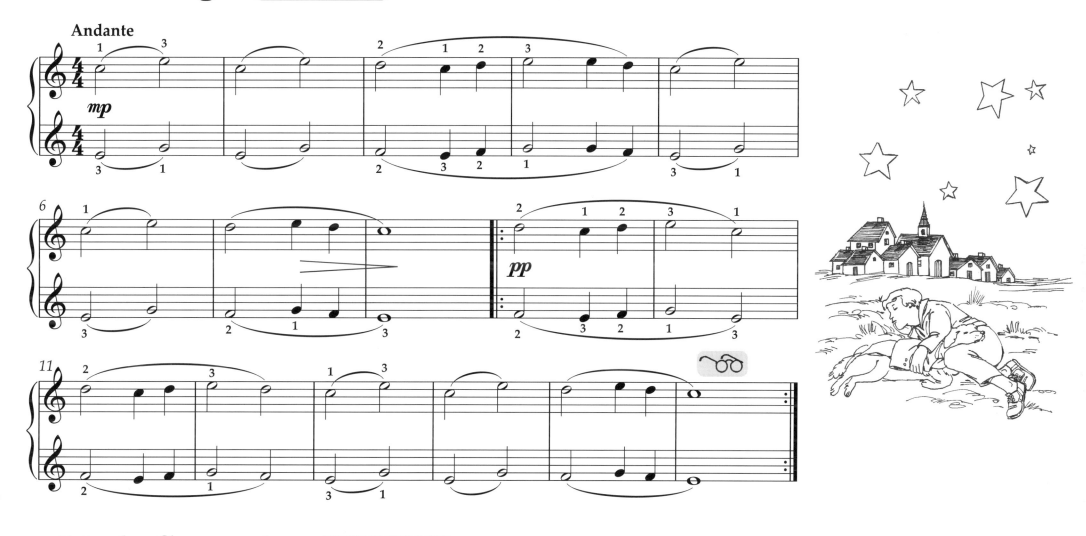

7 Little Cossack

Primo **Pupil**

Traditional

8 Aiken Drum

Secondo | Teacher

Traditional

9 In the pine forest

Secondo | Teacher

Traditional

8 Aiken Drum

Primo · Pupil

Traditional

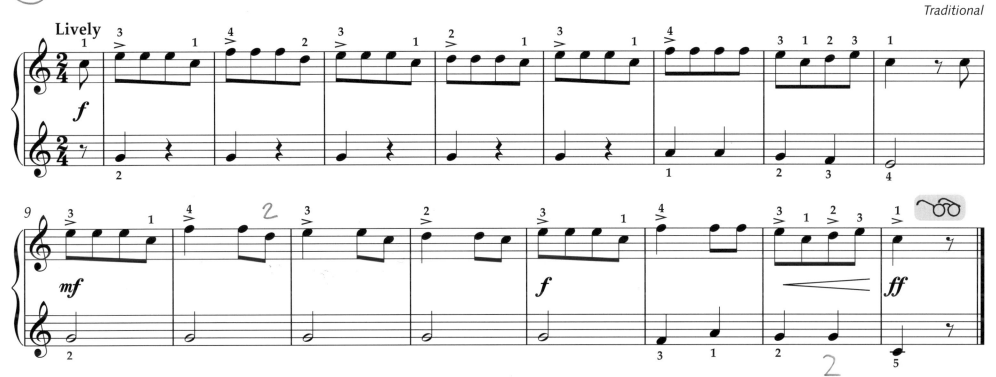

9 In the pine forest

Primo · Pupil

Traditional

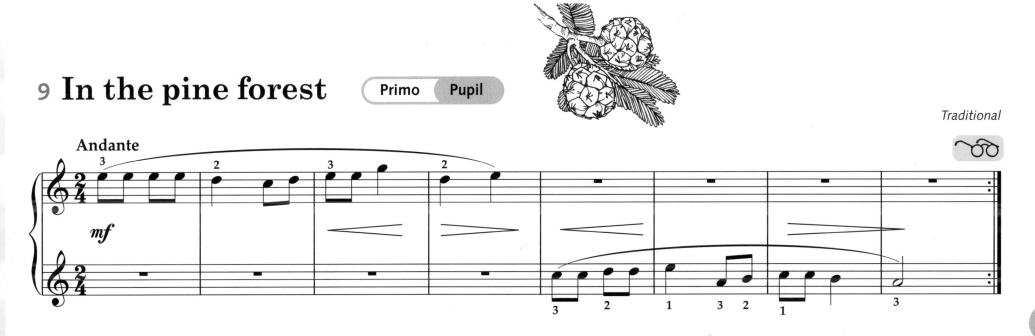

10 Peter's song

Secondo   Teacher

Kabalevsky

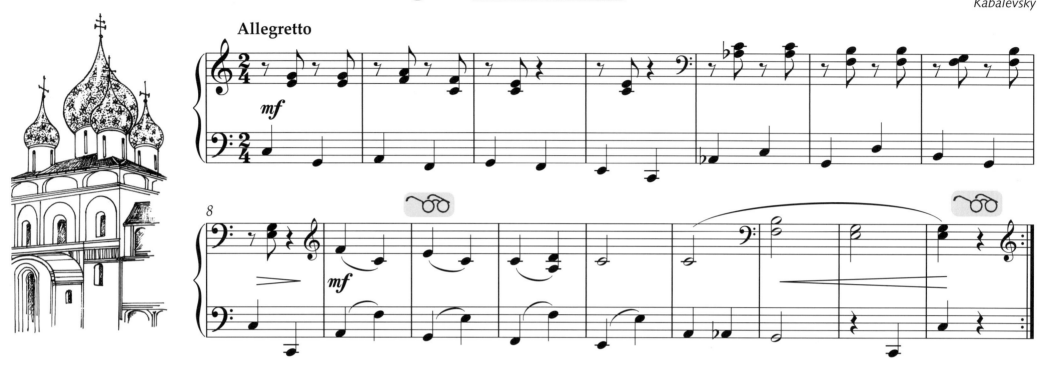

11 I love little pussy

Secondo   Teacher

Traditional

10 Peter's song

Primo **Pupil**

Kabalevsky

11 I love little pussy

Primo **Pupil**

Traditional

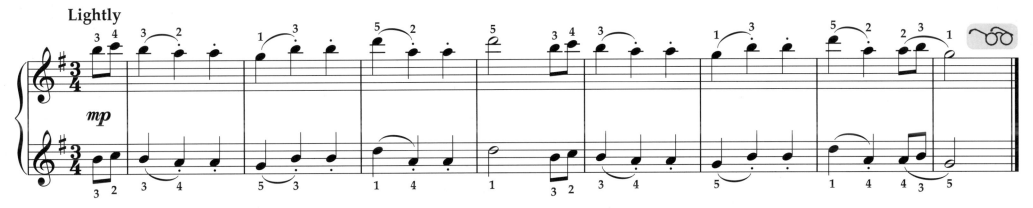

12 Donkey riding

Secondo | Pupil/teacher

Traditional

Trotting along

13 Westminster chimes

Secondo | Pupil/teacher

What time is it? Decide on a time, and make sure your clock strikes the right number of chimes.

12 Donkey riding

Primo / Pupil

Traditional

Trotting along

13 Westminster chimes

Primo / Pupil

'Chime' an extra four bars at the end for four o'clock.

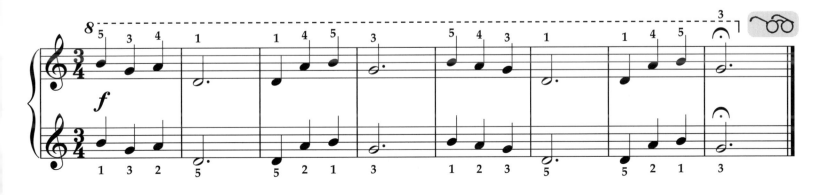

15

14 Floral dance Secondo | Pupil/teacher

Traditional

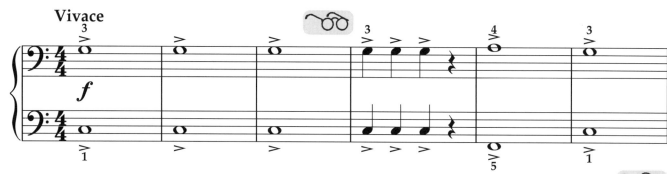

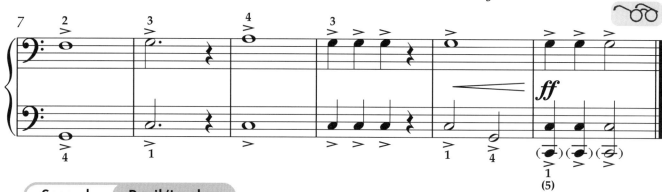

15 Cherry blossoms Secondo | Pupil/teacher

Fanny Waterman

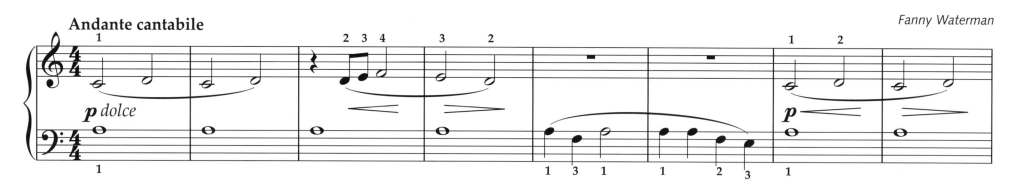

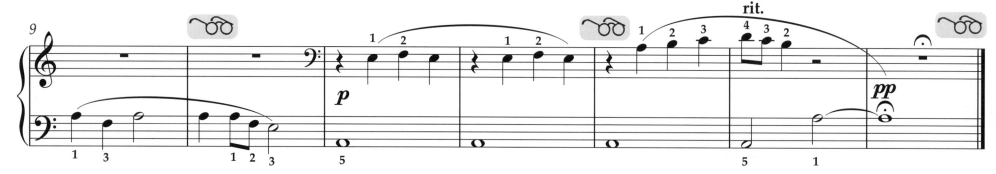

14 Floral dance [Primo | Pupil]

Traditional

15 Cherry blossoms [Primo | Pupil]

Fanny Waterman

16 Springtime

Secondo Teacher

Diabelli

16 Springtime

Diabelli

Grazioso

17 War drums
Secondo   Pupil

Fanny Waterman

18 Underneath the spreading chestnut tree
Secondo   Teacher

Traditional

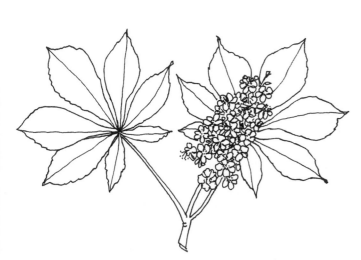

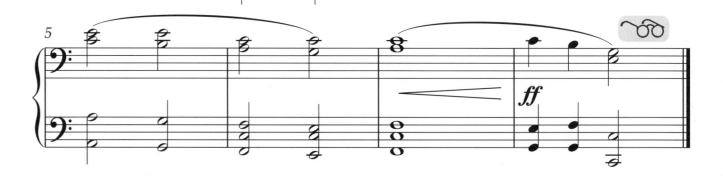

17 War drums

Fanny Waterman

18 Underneath the spreading chestnut tree

Primo Pupil

Traditional

Giocoso

19 Tarantella

Secondo   Pupil/teacher

Fanny Waterman

20 Rule, Britannia!

Secondo   Teacher

Arne

19 Tarantella

Primo · Pupil

Fanny Waterman

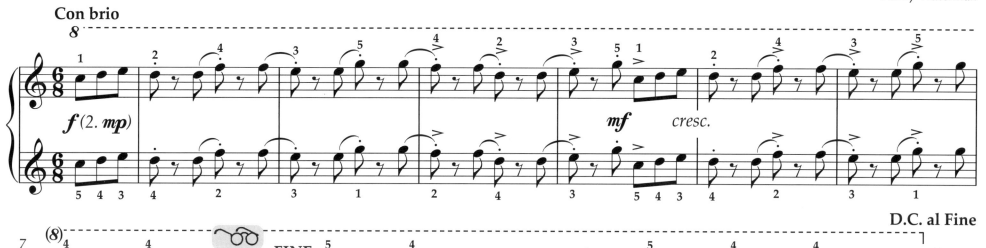

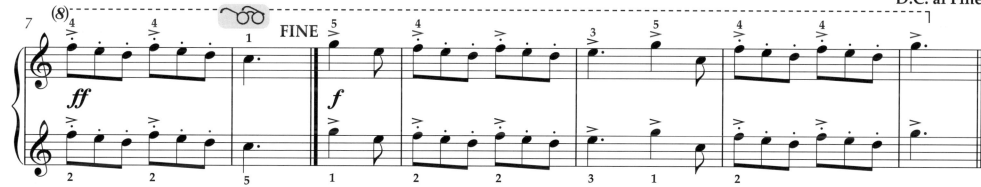

20 Rule, Britannia!

Primo · Pupil

Arne

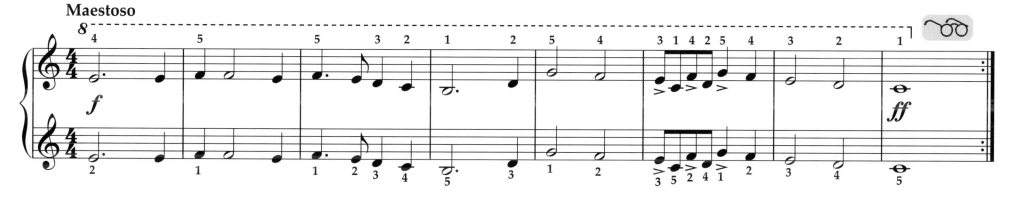

Contents

First published in 1992 by Faber Music Ltd
This edition © 2008 by Faber Music Ltd
Bloomsbury House 74–77 Great Russell Street London WC1B 3DA
Music setting by Jeanne Roberts
Illustrated by Julia Osorno
Cover design by Lydia Merrills-Ashcroft
Page design by Susan Clarke
Printed in England by Caligraving Ltd

ISBN10: 0-571-53203-9
EAN13: 978-0-571-53203-2